TRAVELLING TO ARTISTICA

A Vision Quest

by

4 American Artist

Who held a reverence for the Outdoors

*

4 one man, one act plays

by

Bob Van Lindt

*

Bob Van Lindt

vanlindtClassics

8349 Dongan Ave

Suite 2

Elmhurst, New York

11373

ISBN: 978-1544876634

Cover and book design by CreateSpace
Cover Painting: "Boy Hiker" by the Author
www. bobvanlindt.biz
Back cover photo by Carole Van Lindt

DEDICATION

*

This book of plays is a homage to the American Artists
of the 19th century who held a reverence for the outdoors.
Also thanks to my wife Carole and our loving children
Carson, Susan, Eric and Christian who round
out this affair with interest and support in my writing bliss.
I'd like to also thank to the actor Ray Walsik who played
Winslow Homer and Don McMullen who played Frederick
Remington in my stage production

Contents:

INTRODUCTION

These are 4 plays of American Artists who went to great lengths to pursue their goals and persevere in the wilderness, making sojourns and coming back with Immense coverage on their chosen subjects.

WINSLOW HOMER---His Civil War coverage, rural country life and eventually the sea and the people who made their living from it.

FREDERIC REMINGTON---whose depiction of American Indians and western motifs in paintings and sculptures left behind a legacy of the West.

JOHN JAMES AUDUBON---the bird ornithologist who risked all, family, friends for almost solitude among his beloved winged creatures.

FREDERIC CHURCH----trekking to the far reaches of the Arctic for his large visionary appetite.

WINSLOW BY THE SEA

CAST OF CHARACTERS

WINSLOW HOMER   American Artist of the middle 19th century. Painted rural farm life, Civil War coverage, beautiful women in timeless Illustrations, ending his life with his attention to the people who made their living from the sea.
He was confident, idealistic and determined. A romantic with youthful exuberance

SCENE

His studio in Proust Neck, Maine where he now resides after extensive travelling.

(Homer recounts the war and explains his existence to present day)

TIME   the year is 1910, thereabouts

SETTING: The room contains a couple of easels, artist supplies, and bowls of brushes (can substitute Oriental vases for bowls) equipment (fly rod & creel) + a lobster net from his travels.

AT RISE: Homer stands gazing out window at the sea (contemplating his Life

HOMER

Bringing myself back from the war was something short of a magic trick and
Divine miracle. The horror and slaughter is etched in my memory forever.

The love and peace portrayed in my pictures are a direct result of that aftermath.
I would rather deal with the essence of love than anything negative to the contrary.

Man has brought himself up to par with forces beyond his management. Bringing about destruction anytime he persists is going against the grain of love.

I know, from time to time, he tends to brake his pattern of dissent and contribute immensely to mankind that brings love and joy and wellbeing to all. I believe he is basically the kindest species on earth.

    HOMER folds his arms and walks to center stage

HOMER

I can recall the fateful day at Harper's magazine when Charles Parsons, the Art Director said "Homer! Your work here at Harpers Weekly has been excellent. On a freelance basis you have contributed immensely to the magazine. We've had many letters from our readers complimenting the realism and vitality which you inject into your work.

(Pause)

My colleagues and I would like you to consider a staff position with Harpers along with a generous salary increase of course I answered, "I'm afraid I couldn't accept your offer. I prefer the uncertainty of independence and its reward of absolute freedom. The slavery at the lithography shop in Boston is still too fresh in my recollection to let me care to bind myself again. From the time I took my nose off that litho stone, I have had no master and never shall have any." Even though a tug of war was raging in me I commented, "However I'll stay on as a freelancer."

HOMER

"Well then Homer we have an important assignment for you. As you know our Country is gripped by this Civil War. I don't have to tell you it will be a rough and tough assignment. I've been there. You will be stationed in the field in the thick of the battle. There you will encounter many things---terrible things. There will be heavy artillery explosions all around you and sniper fire, wounded men crying out for help as well as bravery above and beyond the call of duty. Men everywhere as far as the eye can see, sweeping across fields, plummeting down hills----charging with a furor unknown to civilized people in this so-called time. Of course you don't have to take this assignment. We'll understand if you reject it. It's just that we and the readers have need of this kind of reporting. First had illustrations truthful of their nature that only your mind, heart and hand can produce. It's up to you"

(Homer is rolling his eyes at every conjecture)

It certainly sounded dangerous and frightening. My tranquil world was tumbling in my mind. Should I take it up? Up until then I've been in a Dreamscape. It was a thrill to illustrate the skaters in Central Park, the corn huskers of New England and the farm girls I've come to know and love. I could refuse and just bypass altogether but I needed the assignment. My supplies were low and my fishing trips with my brother were an essential part of my life. I had to go. It seemed everyone's duty in those days to contribute to the war's efforts.

HOMER

(Comes to grips)

It seemed just yesterday I was running past fences, over hills, jumping brooks, greeting my mother, father and brother Charles by the door. A quiet time with a cane pole and a can of worms, fishing the many ponds and lakes surrounding our home, where my early artistic achievements were encouraged by my mother, an amateur watercolorist and had the most influence on my art. I watched her graceful hands move the brush across the blank paper leaving shapes of flowers in its path. Of course there was time also for a prank or two, like chasing girls with a frog dangling in my hand or pulling on the girl's apron bows in the school house. Then in my quieter moments laying in the sweet warm meadow grass in Harmony with myself and nature, taking in with the eye the splendor of the trees and rock formations along the stream's edge and climbing the hilltop for a more lofty view.

That feeling of oneness I got from the outdoors has followed me everywhere enticing me with the seductive sights, sounds and smells of the country where a boy could roam free----being a country boy at heart I was not impressed with city life but the job at Harpers Weekly as a freelance illustrator was wide open coverage in town as well as the country.

HOMER

My deep love of nature made me reluctant to have anything to do with the barbaric aspects of the war---the indiscriminate destruction of life----American Life.

(Lights fade slowly. Sounds of marching troops to drummer's beat and a signal is given to charge! The stage explodes with flashing lights as a clash is heard from the opposing armies in combat. As this effect is lowered, a very angry Homer is behind a desk and writing this letter)

"The importance of my assignment in this seemingly senseless

Annihilation of American life becomes increasingly dulled against the sharp clash of tempered sabers. I find it difficult to illustrate the agonizing distorted faces of the dying and those subjected to the butchery of the rusted surgeon's knife.

Therefore, I am requesting immediate transfer to some other illustrative duty In offer to immortalize this ceaseless conflict for future generations."

(Lights fade up with spotlight on Homer. He laments further)

After the war I did less work for Harpers and instead turned my attentions back to painting country life. Ah! the outdoors and the pretty girls who compliment their surroundings so well was given my undivided attention.

HOMER

After the war I did considerably less work for Harpers and instead turned my attentions back to painting country life. Ah! The outdoors and the pretty girls who complement their surroundings so well was given my undivided attention. In fact, my work became intimately preoccupied with women. Their amusements and their fashions. And wherever I could, I joined my brother Charles and my parents at Proust Neck, Maine. Father decided to move the family out of Boston after his loss of the family's fortune in the California Gold Rush.

About the same time I was apprenticed in the lithography shop, where I copied other artist's pictures and photographs, with the shop always getting the credit. It was something of a treadmill existence. Absolutely the worst time of my life. Up until that bloody "every man for himself" Peninsular Campaign skirmish.

However I had no desire to remain anonymous and at every opportune time I smuggled my initials on the stones that I worked on. When I'm left on my own judgment, I can capture that timeless element of simplicity universal to all people, old friends, and familiar faces, something that everyone could relate to, the common denominator of life called humanity. Luckily for me, most publishers familiar with my independent nature gave me free rein.

(Strolling across stage—lights fade on studio)

HOMER

Walking the cliffs at Proust neck allowed me to study the sea, meditate and contemplate the future. I spent the time sketching rural farm life. The haymaker In his sunlit meadow, the plowing, the harvesting and of course the young girls. I found inner contentment and peace. But I sensed a change about my work, with the discovery of the rich medium of watercolor, I discovered a vibrant life, an emotional warmth recaptured, if you will. Not in time though to save me from the events of a dwindling market for my work. A post was fickle trendy American public wasn't buying my earthy country fold and pastoral life Anymore. Reluctantly I had to sell my watercolors at low prices and with Recognition and financial security slow in coming I was waging an inner struggle to continue painting pictures the public didn't want, or to go into the chemical business with my brother Charles. Well, I kept my youthful lyricism and joy in all things of the senses.

Now the time was coming for me to express things more profound than pretty girls, farm boys, and sunny sails on a windy day. My youthful phase in seeing and painting was past. I felt my driving energy and artistic instincts were seeking their proper path. Times were changing. I needed to change. I needed to rediscover a lost part of my soul. It was as restless as the ocean in front of me

9

HOMER

"Wake up you damned pond"

(Homer shaking his cane at the ocean)

I battled discouragement and held on to the hope that the greatest time of growth was about to begin. So I went to Tynemouth England, a popular artist colony.

There ships were hunted daily by cataclysmic storms and slammed and beaten against the rocks. When waves broke on the reefs, they seemed to leap into the clouds like souls stretching for recognition. I saw a relentless struggle and anger of the sea as a reflection of my own restless struggle, a searching to fill the void in my soul and my work. I observed man's struggle against the elements of the fierce sea and watched in fascination at the hardiness of the life-saving brigades launching themselves into the sea in small boats, performing rescue missions that left me staring in wonderment. When I set out for my morning walk through the grey damp dawn, I strolled through a world of women, fisher girls I called them. Going about their tasks, resupplying the boats and coiling the ropes for the next mission. They fascinated me.

HOMER

How different they were from American girls who gathered flowers, played croquet and concerned themselves with the fashions of the day. These were sturdy creatures, handsome in their robustness, yet softly poetic in their breathless anticipation for the safe return of their men. They were truly humane heroes to portray on canvas for all to appreciate.

In the moist English climate, with its cloudy skies and soft grey light, I painted these women gathering the mussels on the beach. Mending the nets, their large Rough hands darting in and out with the same skill the men apply to their Missions. I waited with them on the cliffs, their eyes straining to see the far foggy horizon, anticipating the uncertain return of their men. I sketched them striding across a gale swept beach, their wet clothing caressing their voluptuous curves. Those were courageous women, capable of doing the work designated to them. (Light comes up to reveal his studio surroundings .He is more confident and fulfilled)

Immersed daily in his new design of life, my art underwent a profound change. The wind is now a gale, instead of a gentle breeze, the sky is a moving threatening spectacle of grey clouds, the sea becomes an avenging uncertain element in nature's changing moods that breathes new life into my paintings.

HOMER

(Looking over his English sketch pad)

I've certainly come to know myself and discovered the raw basic element of humanity that lay hidden beneath my brush for so long. The peril of the ocean and the people who make their living from it will be my recurring and dominant theme.

So I choose a solitary life face to face with the Atlantic. The strength and majesty of the sea rush into my work. From this moment on, what I hold closest to my Heart will be in all my paintings. The wildness of the sea. The way that I have chosen gives me the full balance of my life. The sun will not rise or set without my notice and thanks.

(lights fade)

THE END

REMINGTON NOTES

REMINGTON

CAST OF CHARACTERS

FREDERIC REMINGTON   American artist of the late 19th century. A large rugged individual with a strong personality and who has seen adventure on the western plains and recorded Indians and cowboys at work and play as he saw them.

SCENE

Log cabin back east

TIME

The year is 1910

14

REMINGTON

SETTING: A room is filled with mementoes of the West---Indian rugs, Headdresses, bows, etc. There is an easel with canvas in progress on it. General artist's materials are scattered about.

AT RISE: Remington enters cabin with armful of wood. He removes his hat and gloves----looks about the room and his eyes become

Fixed on a sculpture on a tabletop.

(He speaks rather slowly but proud and trying)

Sculpting came to me as a necessity due to a recent decline in sales and a certain success of Charles Russell and Schreyvogel whose backgrounds were similar to mine. So I attempted to throw all my experience and jubilation into my sculpturing. To my surprise and gratification, I came up with a feeling of success. Once again a rush of youth flowed into my bloodstream.

REMINGTON

(He gets excited)

I built a shed-like studio on my Mount Vernon property. There I adopted Bronzing. There were Rough Riders, broncos and lone cowboys in contemplation. The paintings however sat. If only there was time to see them receive their proper due.

(He sits)

Time is slipping away

(He cups his face in his hands for a few moments

And then is rejuvenated in spirit. He stands up)

The cattle drive was long and hot. Sometimes cattle would be dropping like flies. In the thick of the herd, temperatures reached 150 degrees. On day an Indian tried to spook the hot and tired cattle just as they caught wind of water. Cattle could tell there was a hidden spring ten miles away. Well, this Indian hid In some sagebrush and by the time he jumped up and yelped, the cattle had stampeded over him. That's when I decided to take notes on the West.

(Takes off coat, puts on spectacles and goes to easel to review painting in progress)

REMINGTON

The range was more like home to the cattle and creatures of the prairie than man except during sunup and sundown. There's a beauty not to be surpassed—a spectacle of light no painter could achieve unless he had the memory of the Almighty. One minute it was like a watercolor wash, then dark, stars thick like salt sprinkled on a blue cloth napkin. To bundle up in blankets at night was a soothing relief to your body soreness of the day. Sort of a built in massage. Waking up, your lungs filled with the morning air. The capacity to ride another twenty-five miles or so, until camp time again.

(Scanning the work he retrieves notes and sketches)

The woods has always been my other love like the prairie. The hunting, fishing, canoeing all primitive acts that tie man to nature. Not man vs. nature. Catching salmon, trout, and shooting the rapids, tells a man a lot about the mysteries of life. Staying afoot is also a challenge as your journey unfolds with roots and crags and slopes that can trip up a man at any turn. The Adirondacks with its deer, lakes, streams, rivers and caves can take a man down to size and up to his Maker with wonder and awe. Cranes taking flight in the marsh is majestic. Bird sounds akin to paradise. Time in the forest produces an intoxicating aroma of bacon, venison and fish that only man since eternity can identify with.

REMINGTON

(Picks up brush and starts to paint)

Back East, I'd be chopping logs at this time just like here. Only difference is for myself and not for members of the Yale Club. It's just a certain satisfaction a man gets fending for himself. A kind of purpose for living—keeping in touch with the Gods so to speak. The thoughts alone are sacred.

"The sun in this arid country does more than blister my nose". It's an overpowering landscape. Being on the open plains, the rains could come in a flash, just a cloud or two would appear over a hill, then thunder and lightning everywhere, driving cattle through it while keeping your horse steady was tough enough to handle.

Your horse is your best friend on the plains drive, he's in sympathy with you. You can talk to him---keeps a cowboy sane and alerts him to danger.

The Indian on the other hand can travel twenty-five miles on foot if need be—no boredom, no distraction. Just the necessity to hunt, fish and trap in his own element. The prairie showing him signs along the way where a snake is near.

He knows where water is at all times, a knowledge he's had since birth. I once knew this Indian who travelled up a stream in the moonlight as if he was a badger looking for food.

Remington

I befriended that Indian and became a welcome guest at his village. To awaken in the morning with the sunlight streaming through the teepee top is akin to the light Daniel must have witnessed in the lion's den. Pulling back the entrance flap and seeing the women and children preparing the morning food. The Indians tending their horses, all dressed in colored feathers and beadwork, all looking like a sophisticated brand of cave people, who held a reverence for the outdoors.

The cabin I settled in had a large area for cooking with great north light. The main room supplied me with a golden light. That cabin gave me a warmth of living I never had back East. I'd set up my easel to take advantage sometimes of the warmth of the stove. Otherwise the main room supplied me with the sort of light I could envision my subject matter for the day.

A band of Indians attacked my homey abode about sunup one April. They heard there was a rancher who was receiving what was believed to be large shipments of food. After a few man to man shots among us, I parlayed them into becoming my guests. They took to my food like savages on a picnic. They stuffed their game bags too. My cabin with its collection of Indian regalia I used for my drawings brought them to eventual trust.

REMINGTON

The next time I saw them was in June when they dropped an antelope in front of my door. The women and children were standing in parade stance in their finery of leathers and buckskins. They all looked like they were dressed for Sunday Church. I bet they knew more about the Almighty than the average cowpoke. I loved them for themselves, truly I did.

The time of day I painted was any time the zest was there and the zest was always there, for I had these repeated visions of legends, legion of lost patrols that were to be taken seriously as the smoke signals atop the prairie hills. Communication in the West was not to be taken lightly or you might lose your scalp. There was this farmer once who was warned of possible raids on his corn grain. He paid no mind. Well, the next morning he awoke to find his barn stripped of provisions and crows flying all over the place like it was some empty mine shaft.

When you received the news of the day, any hour, any minute, you listened with the upmost clarity---no time for wandering thoughts. Drunken cowboys on the plains soon found out sobering evidence of others before them in their state.

REMINGTON

On the day I left the West to return East--- a feeling of sadness came over me. Due to the rising costs of shipping my art to dealers, my business ventures failing, I decided to return east for the ease and security in which to paint and support my creative habit.

(he is saddened and stops painting, he's gripped by the reality of the daydream)

An era has passed now and I must release the prairie and my cabin with its solitary existence back to the Gods. The silence broken only by the occasional sounds of the small creatures that took refuge near the shade of my hut.

Together with the wind rustling through the trees was like having friends for company. The Indians by then were on reservations and outlaws were being rounded up one by one. People were becoming more civilized, hardly anyone wore guns anymore. Maybe it was the romance of the time. People wanting to live on the edge of the wild, so to speak, the untamed.

I stood at the train depot watching the new pioneers arrive with furnishings, cargo and shipments, all getting ready to do the job of opening up the new frontier. Myself and a few travelling salesmen headed East in the opposite directions-journey through time to the next station in life.

REMINGTON

(He crosses downstage to sit down)

Once again back in illustrating class at the Art Students League in New York, I was aware that some of my friends and colleagues had never been in the field as I was. Nevertheless, some of their work was very good but I always felt they could use a good adventure or two. The models had the necessary anatomy but lacked outdoor Western look I was used to.

But I must not exercise my art with complaint. Because I feel the drawings I have brought back, have a kind of reporting look that only the Western adventure gave me. This has enabled me to sell my drawings profitably and to acquire new assignments

You see I had this trip to Cuba with Teddy Roosevelt and the Rough Riders. This proved to be very exciting. Exotic looking palm trees with sand and earth mixed with wet sea grass dotted the jungle coastline, the enemy all dressed in white hats. The campaign itself was a mystery to me. I bet that sometimes the readers in the states craved too many adventure stories and that editors just drummed up events.

REMINGTON

I made returning visits back to the West again. To Wyoming, New Mexico and Oregon. I did illustrating coverage for Harpers and Collier Magazines. I did coverage on Geronimo's activity and his capture. I always had a sympathetic view toward the Indian and his rights, and I had the blessing of the President of the United States, Teddy Roosevelt.

My ideas of compassion just weren't sound enough for the Authorities to treat the Indians any better. I did however see them put on Reservations.

MY trip to the West has been like a past life revisited and will always continue to be the source of my courage and inspiration.

(Lights fade)

The end

AUDUBON DREAMS

AUDUBON

JOHN JAMES AUDUBON   American Artist of the 18th and 19th century. A dreamer, a lover of birds. He painted directly in the wild with rare beauty not seen until then. An outdoorsman in the tradition of the frontier.

SCENE

Campsite in the woods

TIME

The year is 1826

AUDUBON

SETTING: Campsite----complete with tent or similar shelter, fire pit with coffee pot, haversack, sketch pad and paints. Musket and powder horn hung on a rack made from branches. It is secluded and serene except for the surrounding trees and stars.

AT RISE: John James Audubon is sitting on a log sipping coffee and is in deep thought as if he was contemplating the universe. It is early morning.

(He sips coffee as he looks about and speaks)

I had been at sea only one month captained by a John James Audubon, my guardian who had raised me as a son in the French Colony of Haiti. My father Louis XVI had sent me abroad some fourteen years ago during the French Revolution.

I was on my way home to see my family again, when in the still of the night, a storm took us all by surprise and the ship took on a lot of water. I was put in a small boat and sent adrift as the Captain tipped his hat and the crew battled a losing cause. The ship then sank beneath the bubbling black sea.

(He puts down his coffee and gets up and takes his jacket off the tree limb)

AUDUBON

I soon found out where I was when a mysterious Indian approached me on the sand.
The headdress of cockatoo plumes told me he was a Seminole Indian I had read

about as a cabin boy at sea. I also knew this was the Florida's in the Americas I

landed in. I knew them to be friendly and sharing. I was taken through a woods

adorned with Birds Of Paradise. Feathered creatures of the most hypnotic colors.

They fluttered and flew around me as if in a coronation of flight. Arriving at the

village, I was given a crown of feathers by the chief and welcomed it with delight.

There I stayed until I became of a young man's age ready to journey on. To find a

place in life so to speak for I knew I could not go home again.

(He starts to stitch the torn sleeve on his buckskin jacket)
In that time I learned to make my own clothes out of buckskin and survive in the

elements, feed myself and adore the wilderness in all its glories. My biggest

attraction and distraction has always been birds. As far as I can remember, they

would clamor outside my shuttered windows and become my boyhood friends.

27

AUDUBON

I therefore dedicated my interest to bringing their portraits to a world of appreciation. I am in sheer ecstasy at finding my true life's work. The Indians themselves held me in high regard and supported my love of birds and brought many specimens to my hut, for me to sketch and paint.

Upon leaving the village at 18 years of age, I had accomplished many drawings. About 130 in total. Beautiful Tanagers, Orioles, Hawks, Owls and Red winged Blackbirds with some Canvasback Ducks thrown in.

(Finishes mending jacket)

Outfitted with a canoe I left the village in a hail of cheers and farewell praises. Down the river I went, over the rapids, my mind filled with happiness and a fulfillment of boyhood dreams and expectations. I passed water birds of all sorts. The Great Snowy Egret in his elusive pose of a one leg stance. There were Cranes, Ibises and Storks. I witnessed a band of crows chasing an owl who got himself exposed in the dawn's early light. Big enemy to the owl those crows. They have been known to attack birds larger than hawks.

AUDUBON

Packed with my drawings in a wooden box, in which I would spend days going over them in the quiet drifts and scan the horizon for some civilization that may lay ahead. With my thoughts of my separated home life and the current that drew me down the river, I suddenly realized that the canoe had picked up speed. It was getting rough as a turbulent swift drag swept the canoe aloft with a speed of flight that took me out of my calm and beautiful thoughts to one of panic on the brink of disaster. I had to use all my wits just to stay calm and let guidance take over. Crashing into a rock sent my trunk overboard. Before I could react, the canoe went up in the air and came down with a crash. I managed to grab a passing log while very minute losing my strength out of paralyzing fear.

I soon found myself in a quiet eddy. I was drenched, hurt, hungry and sad, for expectations were shattered as I looked upon the pool with the fragments of my journey sinking beneath my feet. My drawings were nowhere in sight.

(He stands and puts on jacket)

AUDUBON

Fate must be my middle name, for this coastline, later to be known as the Carolinas, was filled with the most exotic birds I've ever encountered. A pristine paradise where I could settle in and make camp—to study and make notes on their habits and habitats.

Recording all the majesty and beauty of their existence and their prime flights of fancy, I soon acquired another portfolio of prints totaling about two dozen studies over a two month period. During that time, coming back to camp after a three day excursion in the field, I found my new collection chewed beyond repair by a pack of field rats that made claim to my homemade chest of thick rawhide and lacing in their search for food. I sat stunned and helpless. I needed to find civilization for my sanity.

(Grabs musket and sling bag packed with sketch materials and goes
Downstage left. Lights dim on campfire area and up on Audubon)

I chose a fork in the road that looked like a trail where I might encounter human life and soon came upon a small hamlet.

AUDUBON

One quick look around, I could see there was a need for some shingles
of advertisement for the store fronts. I applied for the job and was soon knee
deep in wood and orders. In return I got free rent and board. There I met a
woman named Lucy, whom I courted and married. Her loving disposition and love
of my work gave me the support I needed in a companion. She was as fond of
birds and the creatures of Eden as I was. A blessing in disguise, so to speak.

We settled in a cabin I built on the bank of a sunny brook. We had a garden of
wild flowers of primrose, buttercups, curlier daises, bull thistles, bluebells,
forget-me-nots and morning glories. The colors were a natural attraction for the
winged creatures who visited with utmost pleasure to our homey abode. After
recording all the species in the area. I would get restless. It would be time to
trek back into the wilderness for more studies and drawings. By then we had two
children so it was hard to leave but necessary. One other reason was winter was
coming and we needed fresh meat to store us up. It was a twofold journey. It
was lovely and sad to say goodbye to my children who looked more magnificent
than the birds I searched for. But a fixation with nature pulled me forward into
the unknown of the forest.

31

AUDUBON

I picked an unusual trail that seemed to be used by deer. I could tell by the broken branches and hoof prints in the damp ground. It led me winding in and out of brush so thick it was hard to believe deer with their large antlers could penetrate. Nevertheless, I had a sensation that connected me to the wild as I've never felt before. I came out of the dense growth of skunk cabbage to a clearing in the woods that was almost magical. A group of dead trees. still standing after an attack of sulphur that must have blown down from a rock ledge that had an opening into the bowels of the earth. Hundreds of woodpeckers had taken up living quarters and were breathing new life into the trees. I began to sketch and thank God for true gifts along the way. To capture these studies were an immensely blessed event.

(starts to walk across stage)

On one particular morning in a marsh, not far from my hut, I heard a thunderous noise. At first I couldn't see because of the unsettling fog. Having gained footing on a sandy knoll, I began to make out white flashes. Glimpses, if you will, at the flapping of a thousand wings parting the prehistoric scene

AUDUBON

with passages of luminous white plumes belonging to that of the Royal Tern. The only sound was their flight, around and around they flew, like a morning ritual, in their own ecstasy. All I could do was observe the thrill and remember to take notes of the colors of their crowns and wing tips.

I painted my watercolors until the setting sun, to the last rays of light which would enhance my memory into selecting the right color hues. For that collection of images of birds, I also added a company of muskrats, squirrels, otters and chipmunks. The portfolio rounded out my reverence for the outdoors. Later as the light faded from my window, I'd go over my notes of the day's sightings, smoke a pipe and think of my lovely wife and children. For my thoughts of home were at a peak. I sensed a desperation about me. A journey I must survive and pursue.

I thought of the time a Scarlet Tanager appeared on our window sill one morning. He didn't fly away so I fed him some wheat grain and poppy seed and lifted him inside to my drawing table My children sat and stared in awe.

AUDUBON

He whistled and chirped all through the sketching session allowing me to draw his back and side feathers and record the color coding so important for future renderings. Gathering his strength, he was soon fluttering his wings for eventual take off. I thanked him and brought him back to the sill where in a few moments he sang and flew away.

(walks back to campsite and lights come up on site)

The forest can be as enchanting as a spiritual dream as well as a revelation into a beauty unsurpassed, opening up to majestic vistas where from mountain crevices, you can see views of the lower valley.

From the top of one such canyon down to the region below, I could see swooping, screeching and sailing hawks of all sizes and shapes. Broad wings, Red tails, Red Shouldered, rough legged, sharp-skinned and short-tailed. All eyeing each other in what I assumed was a ritual parade of mate choosing or it might be a hawk family yearly reunion or convention.

AUDUBON

(pours the remaining cup of coffee)

The early morning light sprinkled the valley with streaks of sun blaze which backlighted and highlighted the magnificent winged creatures. Some landed and perched themselves as if judges in a kite contest. I was a welcome visitor, too insignificant to pay any mind for I came equipped with only pad and pencil. The scene lasted until midday when a cloud cover moved in. For a change of scenery was needed for both the birds and myself.

High atop the other side of the mountain from one of the ledges, I got a chance to sketch the elusive Eagle in all its glory of flight. Watching as it swooped down to a lake below to catch giant salmon in its talons. On one such successful dive, it was attacked by a band of crows—50-100 of them, diving and startling the giant bird until it got lower and lower to the water. Trying to regrip the fish he crashed into the lake. The salmon struggling again in his own element—the eagle not wanting to let go was dragged under and never surfaced. The crows searched in vain and soon departed.

(pours out coffee and starts to break camp)

AUDUBON

Again I felt I was ready with a new portfolio and could start the journey back. It took me through some exotic marshes of blue and purple tundra mixed with white sand and pastels of sea green dunes.

Seeing my wife and children again was like a dream come true, standing in the doorway just as I had left them three months ago. A joy to behold. While I was away there was news of shipments of Art and Antiques into our town from the big steamers that now came to our growing community. I went down to the docks to see for myself. there were large crates and trunks, bundles of paintings wrapped in heavy burlap tied with rope, with labels addressed to the noblemen of the country.

With no publication sources within my grasp, I started to think that over the sea somewhere there could be a link. A collector, a market, a lover of birds that might be able to do something with my work. Up to now the world had no idea of my existence. I quietly went to find out prices for passage and then to lay out a plan. First, a job to store up provisions for my family, then the big sojourn that I had to take.

(packs up remaining utensils into haversack)

36

AUDUBON

Upon arriving I heard of a huge ball that was being given by a lady known in the art circles as a lover of birds and artists. I received an invitation from one of the passengers I befriended on board the ship. With my portfolio and dressed in buckskin trousers, velvet frock coat and a homemade muslin shirt and string tie, I made my entrance. The Lady Catherine greeted me with open anticipation and led me to her study. There she viewed my work with tears of joy in her eyes.

She was very pleased and happy and wished to purchase my complete portfolio and give me publication sharing. I could hardly believe my ears. I could return home and support my family and continue to contribute my studies and drawings to a publisher with links in the Americas.

I now go in peace, love, friendship and the knowledge that my Bird Art will be in the future domain for all to appreciate.

(he finishes packing and walks offstage)

THE END

CHURCH IN THE VALLEY

CAST OF CHARACTERS

FREDERIC CHURCH American Artist of the 19th Century. An obsessive searcher of images on a monumental scale. An intense, energetic man in his heyday, now shortly before his death. Reflects on his youth and returns to some of that lost excitement.

SCENE

Library room in a large mansion

TIME

Sometime in early spring in the year 1900

CHURCH IN THE VALLEY

SETTING: The stage is surrounded with packing crates used for shipping.

AT RISE: There is an assortment of small and large stacks of books, frames and rolled canvases. Frederic Church is rechecking the items being donated to a Museum. He suffers from a crippling disease in his hands.

Stage is dim lit

CHURCH

Here in the cold, cold night in my warm, warm mansion, the iceberg dreams of my mind melt as my life is cascading down from the Arctic into the Niagara River and over the falls. The years of study in Physics and Plant Biology has not shown me an escape. To bear this alone only presents me with a feeling of remorse. For it seems just yesterday at an exhibit of my huge paintings, people used binoculars to scan the mighty river flows and glaciers in the early morning light. The chatter and awe were enticing as well as appreciated. I've built my mansion here on the upper Hudson River from their accumulative admission and sales.

CHURCH

My complaint is only with the changing times whereupon the future belongs to the extended viewer and not the artist who has pursued his craft, his art, (his love of life) all his life. For now I see no more visions on this plane except those in infinity in which I must return.

(He resumes packing and discovers a telescope, which brings on memory of his youth)

A friend of mine gave me this telescope when I was 18 years of age. A type used by the sentry scouts in the Civil War. My friend had been a collector of Civil War Regalia and with this telescope came charting equipment used for mapmaking. I quickly charted a course to the outer reaches of the Niagara River, where I would revel at the large canvas of infinity to be.

(Lights dim on the crates and lights up on Church. He returns to the lost excitement of his youth)

It was now time for an extravaganza. The search, the hunt, the treasure of the find and the work that follows. All that one feels and thinks and then shapes, that's what I enjoy.

CHURCH

Painting is like constructing the most satisfying composition of music, only

It's on canvas and not on paper. And the music this time turned out to be the

Roar and thunder of the mighty Niagara River.

The tremors I felt in the process were uncanny and unapproachable. The

adventure of the journey as a whole. Climbing the cliffs, witnessing the might

of the river, hearing the roar and viewing it from as many angles as I could

muster up was grand and satisfying.

Surrounded on both sides with greenery, the power produced by the rising

mist had the birds atop the cliffs, swooping up and down, getting their

thermal ecstasy in the process. The painting proved to be one of my finest

and befitting moments. Later on seeing a small reproduction print was the only

time I got a retrospective view of where I have been or gone.

(Walks slowly downstage left)

The light I try to achieve in my work is within the first half hour of sunup.

That clarity of light almost magical, and yet purple in color, lighting itself

on the horizon, like a palette of colors turned full circle, before the

obscuring shadows of the sun.

CHURCH

The exhibit proved very profitable and quickly the earnings were spent on supplies, canvas, wood and more paints. Bought myself some land on this Hudson River where the valley dips and opens to a wide vista reminiscent of the Arctic glow. There's mist that accompanies it every day. A mist almost difficult to capture on canvas but I'm working on it.

If only to meditate and dream the glories that life offers one. A sunrise, a sunset, a good symphony, good laugh, a loving thought, a gladness of spirit, a zest for living, a friend in God.

I courted and married a lovely girl from the valley and set to build my castle on the Hudson hilltop. She is a person giving of herself to my inspiration and wants to share her life with me unremittingly, unselfishly forever, so to speak. Destiny with roses thrown in I'd say.

(Walks across stage to downstage right)

Here in the valley in my castle on the hill, I envision my journeys to be. I have a research library of encyclopedias, maps and geological notes in which I find great pleasure soaking up the knowledge which expands my thoughts to the horizons and dream dreams relative to the size of my large rooms which hold my large canvases.

43

CHURCH

From the view of the Hudson River Valley, I could see the wild expanse of the Cascade Mountains on the opposite shore stretching all the way to the prairies. I keep my library on Physics, Botany and Art together with my microscope in readiness.

Research matter leads me to believe there is a picture reward, a spectacle in size, that would put the Niagara to shame. It revolves around a tale involving a volcano in South America called Cotopaxi. To render a likeness as well as an emotional impact and a capacity of insight, into a place where only a few have been would be the polarity of my desires.

(Goes back to Center Stage near crates—lights up on crates)

I pack my binoculars, paints, easels, canvases and sketch books. I take my food provisions, cases of clothes for those damp dawns, make railroad and ship arrangements, guide contacts and cabin stops. But most likely I will camp at the appropriate foothills to observe and sketch and paint the volcano and its surrounding area.

CHURCH

There are always some paintings that do not sell because they are too small and someone feels he is not getting his money's worth. The larger ones are the most popular and I prefer to keep them on exhibit for a long time and then to retain them in my possession at my castle. For that reason I am also planning to keep those dear little sketches I made in watercolor in the regions of unknown splendor.

Until one is at one with nature, only can the reflection of the Almighty be seen and felt. I hold these truths faithfully, therefore, bringing to my work a kind of realism that only man who is a creature of perfections and appreciation can produce. I hope to show to my fellow man the places and things in this magical-like planet with abiding pleasure, vividness and respect. That there is a love of seeing these wonders of the world.

Of course I'm not the only man trekking across the plains and the great expanse of Iceland. There is the explorer in every man and at this very moment, they are discovering the nooks and crannies of life. I salute them and their mates. I now go to a place afar from the citadel of my mind to a source of inspiration—the incandescent, luminescent, transcendent of time.

(Lights fade on crates and up on Church)

CHURCH

Here in the Arctic where the journey alone is fragmented by frequent stops and starts in an area of desolated range where a man can equate his fate and fortune by sheer delight of wonder and awe. Gigantic icebergs of organic mounds of frozen energy drifting silently in the icy froth. Sketching the needed impressions were especially gratifying for I knew I was one of a few to have a chance to reveal in paintings, the majesty of one of God's truly scenic kingdoms.

Upon returning, I quickly put together a painting so large, it took up my studio wall and was nine months in the making. It was a joy to behold. A wind whipped through the open window and kept me on my toes and redirected my hand holding the brush in all the right places. It was like a spirit of some unknown source speaking to me in the most luminous spectrum I've ever encountered.

(Light returns to normal)

A year after my last exhibit, I contemplate what life has given me. It leaves me breathless in appreciation to have had the courage and insight, strength and stability to venture forth on these journeys of adventure and discovery.

CHURCH

I defy my critics to challenge me on my work by coming along on a trip into the frontiers of the wild and see for themselves the potent excitement and exactness of my renditions. Surely they would come away with a new experience and respect for not only me but for anyone who attempts greatness by merely taking an action. This I hold open to anyone willing to see first hand truth in the making. The nights in my study---releasing the imagination, to creatively visualize the potential in images that could support my claims. Whereupon bringing a collective series of steps to completion by doing instead of dreaming.

But now a crippling disease has cancelled all my trips and most of all, my painting. I ask myself, in what way can I contribute something to humanity. Could I publish a book of memoirs? Can't hold a brush—can't hold a pen! Could I sing a song of praise at church? I was never known for my singing voice—whistle?—yes!

I could whistle symphonies out there in the vast quiet places I visited, it was company as I made sometimes long detailed notes to accompany my sketches. I needed to see which light was best for the finished painting. The early dawn of civilization look or the late afternoon of life's light.

CHURCH

Best be getting back to the notion of contribution. I venture I could empty my castle of large works and dictate my writings, for those who want to travel only in the mind. Until that day, they can and will make the long sojourn into life's wondrous places and learn from the hidden mysteries and gifts to come.

(Lights dim on crates and up on Church)

That day at the Museum when I gave them my work, a feeling of sadness and at the same time, gratification came over me. I realized that giving so that many could enjoy my work and grow rich in their imaginings was indescribable. Now in the museum space where once again people could come in large groups and view and exchange among themselves the majesty and importance of life's wonders. I have been given that chance and I welcome the Final Curtain. Reflecting back as far as memoirs are concerned, they have kept me enriched with occasional details forgotten and once again brought to life so vividly and brilliantly.

The contemplation in my tent at the foot of the Niagara, my thoughts as I witnessed the mountains of icebergs before me in the dawn's early light.

CHURCH

The joy of being the first man to display his sojourns in immense

coverage. My ego has always been in tow, my pleasure has always outgrown

it. My artistic appetite has always been fed.

The extension of a single concept of thought can go a long way into the

future when one puts one's mind to it.

Sooner or later---you too will be led to a discovery.

(Lights fate)

THE END

EPILOGUE

These 4 American Artists have braved the elements and brought their works to the heights of mastery and at the same time brought to light the artist the artistic merits long due them in their quest for life's beauties and wonders of the world. Be it a bird paradise as painted by JOHN JAMES AUDUBON in the wilds of our American forests or the rural farm life depicted by WINSLOW HOMER, interrupted by an assignment to illustrate the Civil War and finally end his days studying the sea, its ominous presence as well as its majesty and the people who make their living by it.

FREDERIC REMINGTON painted the closing West with its rough riders, cowboys and Indians in their finery and way of life. And lastly FREDERIC CHURCH whose magnificent coverage of the unknown regions of the Artic, volcanoes in South America and the mighty Niagara River, has come to bring a new experience to art. I have condensed their life's journeys and sources of inspiration and their relentless spirits to guide you on your Vision Quest in imagination.

www.ingramcontent.com/pod-product-compliance
Lightning Source LLC
Chambersburg PA
CBHW020711180526
45163CB00008B/3034